PARENT GUIDE TO

★USA★

Junior Field Hockey

PARENT GUIDE
TO
USA JUNIOR FIELD HOCKEY

PARENT GUIDE TO

★USA★

Junior Field Hockey

**Rainer Martens, PhD
Director of the
Office of Youth Sports
University of Illinois**

in conjunction with

**The United States
Field Hockey Association**

Human Kinetics Publishers

Publication Director: Richard D. Howell
Copy Editor: Margery Brandfon
Typesetter: Sandra Meier
Text Design and Layout: Lezli Harris
Cover Design and Layout: Jack W. Davis

All photos by Steve Parker, Syracuse, NY, with the exception of the photo on page 34, which was supplied by Susan McNair, and that on page 30, by Wilmer Zehr.

Illustrations on pages 20, 27, 38, 40, and 44 by Gary Lapelle. Illustrations on pages 42, 43, 46, and 49 by Warren Smith.

Library of Congress Catalog Card Number: 81-84644

ISBN: 0-931250-27-7

HUMAN KINETICS PUBLISHERS, INC.
Box 5076
Champaign, Illinois 61820

Contents

Acknowledgments

I would like to thank the USA Field Hockey Association for their help in preparing this guide. I especially wish to acknowledge the young hockey players for their patience and assistance and the coaches, Margaret Martin, Patricia Korta, and Jane Posse, who had fun demonstrating the basics of field hockey to the players. Also, my thanks to Dawn Heckleman and members of the Junior Hockey Committee (Elise Gerich, Karen Hellyer, Sandi Inglis, Tina Sloan-Green, George Tyler, and Nancy Stevens) and Sandra Vanderstoep, Executive Director, USA Field Hockey, for their help.

Foreword

USA Junior Field Hockey has been created to fulfill the need for a quality youth sports program in field hockey. Your child will have the opportunity to play this lifetime Olympic team sport, which is the number two participant team sport in the world. Through the USA Junior Hockey Program, children encounter the challenge of mastering physical, emotional, and social skills that will make them an integral and contributing member of a team as well as society.

The United States Field Hockey Association and the Field Hockey Association of America are concerned about the development of your child in this sport. We know you too are concerned about your role in making this experience beneficial for your child. It is for this reason that this *Parent Guide to USA Junior Field Hockey* has been prepared.

This guide has been designed to enable you to help your child get the most out of his or her involvement. It will also give you a basic understanding of the rules and show you how we reach the goals of the program. The *Parent Guide to USA Junior Field Hockey* will enable you to be actively involved as your child grows and develops through the new challenges and experiences that USA Junior Field Hockey provides.

Mickey Korta
Junior Hockey Director
USA Field Hockey

1

The Sport of Field Hockey

Welcome to USA Junior Field Hockey. We are delighted that your child has decided to play this fascinating Olympic stick and ball sport. Your young athlete will learn the challenge of mastering skills and the discipline of fitting into a team as an integral, contributing member.

We hope that you will become a part of your child's involvement in USA Junior Field Hockey. You'll need a basic understanding of the game to grasp what you see during matches, because your attitude, knowledge, and positive support are instrumental to his or her performance. Therefore, this guide is written to do the following:

- To present to you the basics of USA Junior Field Hockey,
- To clarify what safety precautions are taken to protect your child while involved in USA Junior Hockey, and
- To inform you of your responsibilities.

Regardless of how much you know about field hockey, you will find the information in this guide helpful.

SOME BACKGROUND

Field Hockey and its off-season counterpart, indoor hockey, is an international sport with a tremendous following in every country in which it's played. Brought to England from India at the end of the 19th century, it quickly became the national sport for women. It spread through Europe, gaining popularity with both sexes. American women first played field hockey in 1901, and the sport was introduced to American men a few years later. The United States is unique in that here field hockey is predominantly a women's sport, with men making up less than 10% of the total playing population.

One question frequently asked by newcomers to field

Figure 1—This player is equipped with a USA Junior Hockey stick and ball.

hockey is, "What are the differences between field hockey and ice hockey?" These games do have similarities—both have soccer-based strategy and team formation and both are played with sticks. But beyond these similarities, the differences are numerous. Field hockey's stick is shorter, smaller, and has a hooked end. The game is played using only the flat side of the stick and with a ball instead of a puck. These make playing style and the types of moves executed different from those of ice hockey. Figure 1 shows the field hockey stick and ball as used in games.

Field hockey also has another peculiarity, the obstruction rule. In other sports, protecting the ball from opponents is expected, but in field hockey, that sheltering with the stick or part of the body is illegal and referred to as obstruction (see Figure 2). Every player has a fair and honorable chance at the ball.

Field hockey is one of the few strictly amateur international sports. Both men's and women's field hockey are Olympic sports, with women gaining their slot in the Olympic venue in 1980 for the ill-fated Moscow Games. The USA Men's Field Hockey Team first played in the 1932 Los Angeles Olympic Games.

Figure 2—In this instance, the umpire would call obstruction because the opponent is being sheltered from the ball.

One million youngsters are expected to be part of the USA Junior Field Hockey Program by 1984. We are pleased that you and your child will be part of it—we're proud of our program and are sure that you will be too!

WHY FIELD HOCKEY?

Why do kids want to play hockey? What exactly do they get out of it? There obviously are many different reasons. One of the most important things for both parents and coaches to keep in mind is that not every child picks up a hockey stick for the same reason. One child may want nothing less than the glory of an Olympic gold medal, whereas another is quite happy to be on the team enjoying the friendship of peers. The USA Junior Field Hockey Program has room for all types of players.

For the boy or girl who wants to excel—to discover his or her full potential—USA Junior Field Hockey provides an opportunity to do so. Some of the most satisfying and beneficial experiences for young people can arise when they are intensely involved in and committed to the pursuit of excellence. Today, children have few opportunities to make such a commitment, but increasing numbers of young people are finding that sports provide such challenges. For this reason, sports may be important in helping young people become adults. We hope that your child finds field hockey to be worthy of his or her best effort.

USA Junior Field Hockey is also for the child who places more emphasis on playing a game with friends. Many youngsters do not have the talent to be a champion, or simply are not ready to find out. For these young people, the joy of being with friends, mastering basic skills, and having a good time is more than sufficient reward. In short, we hope that your child seeks the "highs" found in playing field hockey, rather than those that can be purchased on the street. We believe that the fruits of this pursuit will be many.

USA Junior Field Hockey strives to meet the needs of all types of young people. Doing so requires that coaches never forget the uniqueness of players and that they plan the programs to meet these individual needs as best as possible. If your child's coach forgets this, perhaps you should ask her or him to reread this section.

THE VALUE OF FIELD HOCKEY

We think that field hockey has the potential to help the total development of your child. Obviously, we expect fitness (i.e., strength, endurance, coordination, and flexibility) to improve and we hope to instill a desire to continue to be fit throughout life. We also expect players to become more coordinated and better skilled—with skills that not only will help make youngsters better players, but help them in learning other skills. And we dare hope for even more. Especially with your help, we hope that field hockey will contribute to the development of your child's
- sense of achievement
- positive self-concept
- appreciation for what the body can do
- leadership skills
- ability to work as part of a team
- self-reliance
- emotional stability
- social skills
- strong moral code

Yes, we're a bit idealistic, and we know that simply stating these as objectives is no guarantee that every child in the program will achieve any or all of them. Nor do we think field hockey is the only way your child can learn these things. Our point is that these objectives *can* be realized through field hockey but only with the combined efforts of skilled coaches and dedicated parents who understand the needs, aspirations, and limitations of young athletes. And, of course, they can be realized only if young athletes are willing to make the commitment. This is *our* challenge—you, the parent, and we, the coaches—to help your child know the joy of field hockey while she or he matures into a contributing member of society.

USA JUNIOR FIELD HOCKEY PROGRAM

USA Junior Field Hockey is administered through the

United States Field Hockey Association (USFHA) with the support of the Field Hockey Association of America (FHAA). The USFHA and the FHAA are the US Olympic Committee-appointed national governing bodies for women's and men's field hockey, respectively.

As national governing bodies, USFHA and FHAA are concerned with every aspect of the sport of field hockey. This includes player development; umpire/coach training; Olympic team selection, training, and outfitting; event management; sport promotion; publications and technical materials; and the general administration necessary for any nationwide organization having tens of thousands of members. Both the USFHA and FHAA have their national offices at the Olympic Training Center in Colorado Springs, Colorado.

Although USA Junior Field Hockey is under the direction of USFHA, local programs have the flexibility to adapt the program as best fits their own needs and interests. Because of this, it is difficult to describe the actual program in which your child will participate. Some teams will play indoors on a gym floor, some outside on a grass field, or some on a macadam surface. Programs begin not only in the fall during the traditional field hockey season but also in the summer, spring, and winter.

Some things, however, are consistent throughout all USA Junior Hockey Programs. The assignment of players to leagues according to age is one of those standards. As shown in Table 1, the age range within each league is narrow; this is to help ensure your child's safety on the playing field. Although children of the same age still differ in their size and

Table 1 - Levels of Junior Field Hockey

League	Age	Length of half
Rookies	8-9 years	10 minutes
Juniors	10-11 years	15 minutes
Seniors	12-13 years	20 minutes

strength, the narrow age range helps to eliminate any potential difficulty.

Safety rules are also consistent in all programs. For further explanation, see the section on "Safety." Rules are also standard through the USA Junior Field Hockey Program. Rules and safety guidelines were especially developed to make field hockey easy to learn, fun to play, and of course, safe.

Each year during the Thanksgiving holidays, USA Junior Field Hockey is showcased at USA Field Hockey's Hockey Festival. One team is invited from each league (i.e., Rookies) in each local program to participate in the tournament. Local programs may also decide to hold tournaments organized on a local, regional, or even state level. Tournaments are not emphasized in USA Junior Field Hockey, especially those to create All-Star teams, because the major thrust of the program is to teach skills and to make sure all youngsters have a fair chance to play.

EQUIPMENT

Field hockey is a comparatively inexpensive sport to play. Necessary equipment consists of a stick, ball, shin guards, and a mouth guard, as shown in Figure 3. Apparel and equipment packages are available through USA Junior Field Hockey. With registration in the program, your child automatically receives the apparel package. It consists of the following:

- T-Shirt in team color
- Stirrup socks, matching color
- Shin and mouth guards
- USA Field Hockey membership
- Accident insurance—medical and dental

Field hockey equipment is also available in many sporting goods stores. The coach can help you decide what kind of stick is best. No special shoes are needed, just well-fitting sneakers. T-shirts and shorts are fine for practice and games; if the team has color specifications, the coach will let you and your young player know.

Figure 3—This player is fully equipped to play in USA Junior Hockey.

SAFETY

Although playing field hockey results in few serious injuries, minor muscle pulls and strains as well as bumps and bruises do occur. Your child's safety is a prime concern to us, so here are some of the things we do to make hockey as safe as possible.

1. We make sure your child has good equipment and that it is used properly (see "Equipment").

2. We make certain that your child is in proper physical condition to learn field hockey skills and to begin to play in a game.

3. We have modified the rules of the game to make it safer and easier to learn. Players are not allowed to lift the stick above the shoulder or to hit or kick the ball so as to be dangerous.

4. We recruit competent officials who not only enforce the rules but who are trained to prevent injuries by anticipating and stopping potentially dangerous situations.

5. We match children in practice and game situations with players of similar age and playing experience.

6. We strive to have competent, certified coaches who use established, safe procedures for teaching skills.

7. We require players to heed basic safety rules of the team for we know injuries occur most often when children are "horsing around" or are fatigued. Players must wear mouth and shin guards whenever they play.

8. In case of injury, a planned course of action is put into operation to obtain the speediest medical attention possible. All coaches are urged to have a first-aid kit at their disposal and to know how to use it.

9. The USA Junior Field Hockey Program conducts coaching clinics to improve coaches' knowledge of sports medicine, sport physiology, and sport psychology.

10. Finally, we encourage you to impress on your child the importance of following safety rules, and we welcome your suggestions for making USA Junior Field Hockey safer.

THE GAME

As stated earlier, you will gain a greater appreciation for what your child is learning when you understand the movements and strategies that are part of the game. As you learn about field hockey, you will find that what appeared to be disorganized actions, sometimes bordering on chaos, will become well-defined movements having great purpose.

The basic objective of playing field hockey, whether in an Olympic gold medal game or in a Saturday morning Junior League, is to score a goal, or if one's team is on the defensive, to prevent the other team from scoring. A goal is scored when the ball passes between the cones or goal posts at the end line. Goals are given one point, and making a goal is the only way that points are awarded. The scores in your child's game will tend to be quite high, whereas in collegiate and international competition, they are considerably lower (e.g., 2-1, 1-0, 3-2). Also, ties are not broken in USA Junior Field Hockey.

Five youngsters play on the field at a time, but as many as 10 people may be on the team. The size of the field or playing area is a great deal smaller than a regulation hockey pitch (field). The dimensions and necessary markings on the field

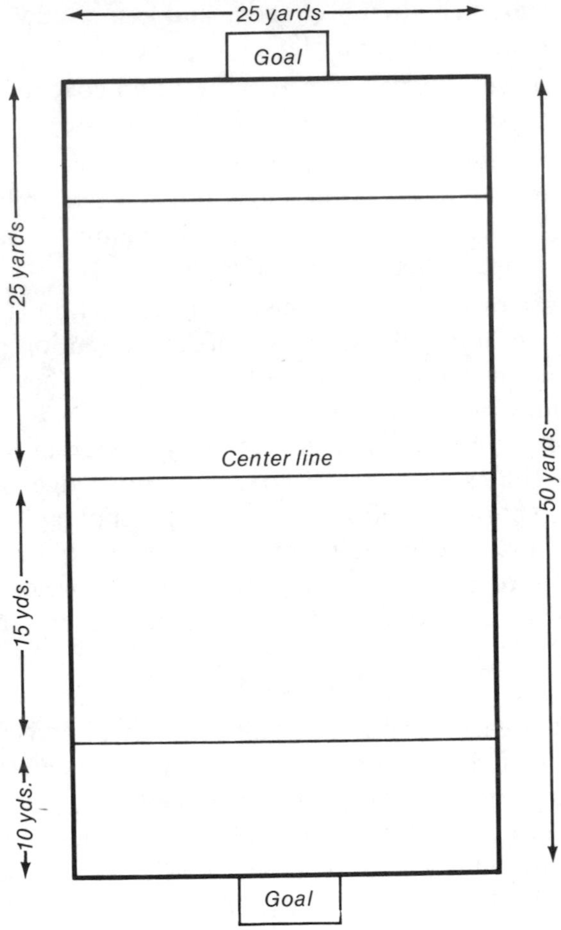

Figure 4—A regulation field hockey pitch.

hockey field are shown in Figure 4.

The field hockey game is divided into two halves. The actual length of the half depends upon the age level of the players. To assure that no girl or boy "warms the bench" all season, all players must play at least half of the game. Unlimited substitution is allowed in USA junior hockey as long as the players are acknowledged by the umpire.

Before the game begins, the umpire meets with coaches and players to answer any questions about the rules, to check sticks for safety (see Figure 5), to make sure all players are wearing mouth and shin guards, and to determine who begins

Figure 5—The umpire will check the sticks before the game to make sure they are safe.

the game. Team captains call the toss of the coin, and the winner of the toss chooses between having the advantage of the "pass back" (read on for an explanation) or the goal they would like to defend. In the second half, the teams trade goals, and the team who did not have the advantage of the "pass back" at the beginning of the game now starts.

A "pass back" is the opening move—one member of the starting team stands on the center line facing the opponent's goal. This player then passes the ball back to a team member, setting the ball "in play" as soon as the first team member touches it.

Field hockey is similar to soccer in strategy. A match consists of a series of one-on-one confrontations for possession of the ball. These confrontations occur within a framework of team effort, defense, and attack. That teamwork is shown in the passing and receiving of the ball that are essential parts of the game.

The ball moves up and down the field (or court) in a variety of ways. Some methods—kicking, throwing, or driving

Figure 6—The grip used in dribbling and passing.

(similar to the golf swing)—are not allowed. Dribbling is the most common method of propelling the ball. When dribbling, the player taps the ball with the flat side of the stick. The left hand grasps the stick from the top, and the right hand holds the stick several inches below the left (see Figure 6). All players play with the left hand on top of the stick.

Straight dribbling, as shown in Figure 7, is used when a player has a clear field ahead. Control is the most essential skill in keeping possession of the ball. If players are nearby trying to take the ball away (this is called tackling and will be explained later), then another type of dribbling is used.

The zig-zag or Indian dribble is more difficult to tackle than the straight dribble. It is a combination of a forward tap to the left and a "reverse stick" tap to the right. To play the

Figure 7—The straight dribble is one type of dribble.

ball on the left side of the body, the player turns the left wrist over the top of the ball, facing the flat side of the stick to the right (see Figure 8). Again, remember that the ball can only be hit by the flat side of the stick.

Passing is the other way the ball moves during a game. In school and international competition, a variety of different hits are used to pass the ball, but in the interests of safety and simplicity, only a push pass is used in the USA Junior Field Hockey Program. Because of the small playing area, a more forceful pass is unnecessary. In a push pass, the stick is placed directly behind the ball, and the right wrist gives a fast push forward as the left hand pulls back the top of the stick (see Figure 9).

In addition to learning individual skills, USA Junior Field Hockey players learn to apply them to game strategy situations. On an individual level, they learn to dribble, tackle, and dodge other opponents. Tackling is a defensive skill; a

Figure 8—A "reverse stick" is used to play the ball on the left side of the body.

Figure 9—The push pass is the only pass used in Junior Hockey.

Figure 10a—In making a successful tackle . . .

Figure 10b—. . . the defensive player must take the ball away and be in possession of the ball.

player takes the ball away from someone else, as shown in Figures 10a and 10b. A successful tackle is accomplished when the ball is not just hit but taken away from a player, leaving the tackler in possession of the ball. Dodging is used when the player in possession of the ball must get around a defensive player to remain in possession (see Figures 11 and 12).

On a team level, players work together to score goals (offense) and to prevent the other team from scoring (defense). Players may be designated as forwards or backs, each having specific roles and areas of the field to cover. Shown in Figure 13 are typical zones for specific players. As stated earlier, the scores in Junior Field Hockey tend to be quite high, and this is because there is no goalkeeper at this level. One important thing to remember is that coaches in your local program have the option to use different strategies from those covered here, depending upon the strengths and weaknesses of their team.

Defensive play means that the team does not have possession of the ball. There are two basic types of defense used in field hockey; your child's program will be a variation of these. Zone defense is used when players are responsible for the defense of a particular area of the field, whereas person-

Figure 11—To dodge her opponent, the player performs a reverse stick dribble to the right.

Figure 12—After moving to the right of the opponent, the player must quickly move forward with the ball past the opponent.

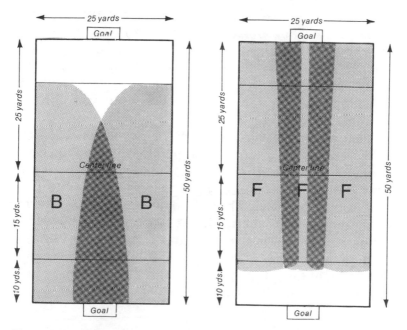

Figure 13—Areas of responsibility for half backs and forwards.

Figure 14—Here the umpire has called obstruction.

to-person defense is when a player is responsible for another player's offensive play.

If a player fouls—uses an illegal hit, performs a move dangerous to another player, and so on—the other team takes a free push at the spot where the foul occurred. If a ball goes over the sideline, it is put into play by the opposing team from the place where it went out. If a ball goes out over an endline and a goal is not scored, the ball is put back into play from the 10-yard line.

When the umpire calls a foul, she or he will blow the whistle and explain the reason for stopping play (see Figure 14). Your reaction to the umpire's calls is very important—children learn how to react to authority figures from their parents' behavior. The time to question a call is after the game, and with politeness. All games are umpired by specially trained people who have the qualities necessary to be a good umpire (a sense of humor, firmness, and a good knowledge of the rules). The umpires are there to ensure fair play and your child's safety.

2
Your Child's Coach

Coaching field hockey offers tremendous challenges and enormous responsibilities. As a parent of a young hockey player, you should determine whether your youngster's coach is capable of meeting the challenges and fulfilling the responsibilities. If the coach does not seem to know what he or she is doing, does not take reasonable safety precautions, or does not teach the same values you try to teach your child, then you should not permit your child to play hockey under this person. But if you are satisfied that the coach is competent, that his or her motives are positive, and that the experience will be beneficial for your child, then you have the obligation to give the coach your trust, support, and assistance without interfering.

Of course, we cannot tell you about your child's particular coach; you will need to find that out. We can tell you, however, something about the coaches in the USA Junior Hockey Program in general. They come from all walks of life, motivated by their love of field hockey and their desire to

During a practice, the coach points to where the next pass should go.

The coach demonstrates how to grip the stick as the players look on.

teach young people this sport. All Junior Hockey coaches are volunteers; many are parents of children participating in the program who donate many hours a week throughout the season to coach your child and, of course, do this for no pay.

The rewards of coaching come in many ways: For instance, coaches experience the thrill of seeing young people master the sport and at the same time gain self-respect and respect for others. Certainly, coaches also appreciate kind words from parents, former participants, and the citizens of the community. Youth coaches all across the country make an important contribution not only to the physical but psychological and social development of young people.

Unfortunately, as in any human endeavor, there are a few "bad apples" in the coaching business. USA Junior Hockey does all it can to eliminate them (or re-educate them), but once in a while a poor coach escapes detection. Thus, it is important that you make sure your child's coach is acting in your youngster's best interest.

On the next two pages is a list of things you should find out about the person with whom you are going to entrust the very life of your child.

COACH EVALUATION CHECKLIST

Coaching Philosophy

☐ Does the coach keep winning and losing in perspective, or is this person a win-at-all-costs coach?
☐ Does the coach make sure that learning hockey is fun?

Motives

☐ What are the coach's motives for coaching?
☐ Does the coach seek personal recognition at the expense of the kids?

Knowledge

☐ Does the coach know the rules and skills of the sport?
☐ Does the coach know *how* to teach those skills
   to *youngsters?*

Leadership

☐ Does the coach permit the players to share in the leadership and decision-making, or does s/he call all the
   shots?
☐ Is leadership built on intimidation or mutual respect?

Self-Control

☐ Does the coach display the self-control expected of the
   athletes, or does s/he fly off the handle at times?
☐ When kids fail, does the coach build them up or put
   them down?

Understanding

☐ Is the coach sensitive to the emotions of the players, or
   so wrapped up in doing his/her thing that their feelings
   are forgotten?
☐ Does the coach have an understanding of the unique
   make-up of each child, and treat each accordingly?

*At the end of a practice session, the players relax while the coach reviews a
few major points.*

It's very rewarding to see your children excited after a game of junior hockey.

Communication

☐ Does the coach's words and actions communicate positive or negative feelings?
☐ Does the coach know when to talk and when to listen?

Consistency

☐ Does the coach punish one youngster and not another for the same misbehavior?
☐ Is the coach hypocritical, saying one thing and then doing another?

Respect

☐ Do the players respect and listen to what the coach says?
☐ Do the players look up to the coach as a person to emulate?

Enthusiasm

☐ Does the coach demonstrate enthusiasm for coaching hockey?
☐ Does the coach build enthusiasm among the players?

Remember—no coach will be perfect (just as you are not a perfect parent), but you need to be satisfied that your child's coach meets some minimum standards. To learn about this person, meet with and talk to other players' parents who know him or her. Don't feel you are snooping; you are fulfilling your obligations as a responsible parent!

THE INGREDIENTS OF GOOD COACHING

We encourage you to take a look at your youngster's coach, but we also want you to appreciate the difficulty of being a coach. Some people seem to believe that the only qualifications needed to be a coach is to have played the sport—and the better a person played, the better coach that person will supposedly be.

The ingredients that make a good field hockey coach, however, include much more than simply having been a field hockey player. In addition to knowing the sport, a good coach must know something about kids. The coach must know about the physical development of boys and girls—what they are and are not capable of doing. A good coach must know about differences in personality—that what is right for one youngster is not necessarily right for another, or even for the same child in a different situation. A good hockey coach must be an astute teacher, a clever psychologist, a pragmatic philosopher, and a shrewd businessperson.

Another misconception in our society is that a successful coach is a winning coach. *Successful coaches do more, much more, than merely win.* Winning is the immediate, short-term

"They said this would be easy!"

goal of every contest, and both the coach and player should seek the prize of victory. To do less is to be a dishonest competitor. But truly successful coaches consider winning to be a by-product in the achievement of more important long-term goals.

Successful coaches place great importance on teaching the fundamentals of hockey well so that boys and girls have the basis for developing their capabilities to the fullest in future years. Successful coaches teach youngsters the satisfaction of striving for excellence, regardless of the outcome. They teach them to enjoy success and to respond to failure with renewed determination, and they help children develop positive attitudes toward themselves. Successful coaches help youngsters learn standards of conduct acceptable to society.

The value of hockey for each child depends a great deal on the coach's sense of values. The successful coach is one who conveys:

- The value of time
- The meaning of effort
- The dignity of humility
- The worth of character
- The power of kindness
- The wisdom of honesty
- The influence of example

When passing to a teammate, the ball should be projected to the space ahead of the player so as not to interfere with the speed of the receiver.

- The rewards of cooperation
- The virtue of patience
- The joy of competition

The challenge of coaching is to make some progress toward conveying these values while striving for victory, and not diminishing any of the fun inherent in field hockey. Coaches sometimes forget that fun is the mortar of a successful hockey experience. Without fun, youngsters turn their interest elsewhere or refuse to make the commitment needed to realize these values. It is the false importance that coaches give to winning that almost always threatens to obliterate the fun in hockey.

Unfortunately, it is not easy to be a coach in a society that defines success synonymously with winning. It is not easy to resist a "winning is everything" philosophy when surrounded by high school, college, and pro sports where winning *is* apparently everything. And it is not easy to keep winning in perspective when parents constantly want their youngsters to win. Yet that is what a *good* coach must do.

HOW YOU CAN HELP

No doubt, being a coach of 20 or 30 energetic young boys or girls is a difficult job. You can help make that job a bit easier, as well as help the kids obtain the full benefit of hockey, by doing the following things:

1. Let your son or daughter know you support their participation in hockey.
2. Provide your child with the proper equipment and encourage its correct use.
3. Monitor your child's hockey participation so that you know how your child is developing.
4. Do not interfere with the coach unless the coach has clearly erred.
5. Keep the coach informed if your child is injured or ill.
6. Make certain your youngster is sleeping and eating properly.
7. Help the coach when asked to do so. You might be needed to raise funds, drive kids to games, keep score or time at a game, or even become an assistant coach. (We have another book for you to read if you decide to become an assistant coach.[1])
8. Keep control of yourself—show by your example how you want your child to behave on and off the field.

---

[1]The book is *Coaching Young Athletes* written by Rainer Martens, Robert Christina, John Harvey, Jr., and Brian Sharkey and is available from Human Kinetics Publishers, Box 5076, Champaign, IL 61820, for $12.

3
Understanding Yourself

As coaches, we have told you about ourselves and our philosophy—our views about the importance of winning, having fun, and your child's happiness. We have suggested how you may evaluate us as coaches. Now, where do you stand, and how will your outlook and actions affect your young hockey player?

Are you able to keep winning in perspective? You might answer with a confident yes, but will you be able to do so when it is your child who is winning or losing, when your child is treated a bit roughly by someone on the other team, or when the umpire makes a judgement against him or her? Parents are sometimes unprepared for the powerful emotions they experience when watching their sons and daughters compete.

One reason that parents' emotions run so high is that they want their child to do well; it reflects on them. They also may believe that their child's failure is their own. Parents need to realize that the dreams of glory they have for their young player are not completely unselfish. But they also should know that these feelings are completely human. Parents who are aware of their own pride, who are even capable of being amused by their imperfections, will keep themselves well under control.

Flying off the handle at games or straining relations with the coach or other parents makes it just that much more difficult for your child. Just as you don't want your daughter or son to embarrass you, don't embarrass your youngster.

It's no secret that kids imitate their parents. In addition, they absorb the attitudes they think lie behind their parents' actions. As you go through the hockey season with your child, be a positive model. How can you expect your daughter to develop a healthy perspective about competing and winning if you display an unhealthy one? Remember—USA Junior Field Hockey is supposed to be a fun experience for your child, and one in which he or she will learn some athletic skills. Winning will take care of itself.

Some parents seem to think that the principles of child rearing do not apply when their child is participating in sports. However, just as your youngster's home, school, and religious environment affect the type of person he or she will be, so does the sports environment. Remember this:

> If your child lives with criticism, he learns to condemn.
> If your child lives with hostility, he learns to fight.
> If your child lives with fear, he learns to be apprehensive.
> If your child lives with encouragement, he learns to be confident.
> If your child lives with praise, he learns to be appreciative.
> If your child lives with approval, he learns to like himself.
> If your child lives with recognition, he learns to have a goal.
> If your child lives with honesty, he learns what trust is.[1]

Here is a checklist you should consider when your child begins playing hockey. If you can honestly answer yes to all the questions, you will find little trouble ahead.

---

[1]Abridged from a "Great Projects Report" which was reprinted in the *Baltimore Bulletin of Education*, 1965-66, **42**(3).

"Can you accept your child's triumphs and disappointments?"

Can you give your boy or girl up?

That means trusting the coach to guide your child's hockey experiences. It means accepting the coach's authority and the fact that he or she may have some of the youngster's admiration that once was directed toward you.

Can you admit your shortcomings?

Sometimes we err as parents, our emotions speak before we think. We judge our child too hastily, perhaps only to learn later that the child's actions were justified. It takes character for parents to admit they made a mistake and to discuss it with their child.

Can you accept your child's triumphs?

This sounds much easier than it actually is. Some parents do not realize it, but fathers in particular are competitive with their sons. If a boy does well in a game, his father may dwell on the minor mistakes, describe how an older brother did even better, or if he had been a hockey player, describe how "Dad did it way back when."

Can you accept your child's disappointments?

Sometimes being a parent means being a target for a child's anger and frustration. It goes along with the job. Accepting your child's disappointment also means watching your youngster play poorly during a game when all of his or her friends succeed, or not being embarrassed into anger when your 10-year-old breaks into tears after a failure.

Can you give your child some time?

Some parents are very busy, even though they are interested in their youngster's participation and want to en-

courage him or her. Probably the best solution is never to promise more than you can deliver. Ask about your child's field hockey experiences and make every effort to watch at least some matches during the season.

Can you let your child make his or her own decisions?

This is an essential part of any youngster's growing up, and it is a real challenge to parents. It means offering suggestions and guidance, but finally, within reasonable limits, letting the child go his or her own way. All parents have ambitions for their children, but parents must accept the fact that they cannot mold their children's lives. Field hockey offers parents a minor initiation into the major process of letting go.

The following letter[2] from a young hockey player to her parents is a poignant reminder of how youngsters view their parents' behavior during their sport participation—and how they are affected by that behavior.

[2]Adapted from a letter which appeared in *You and Your Child in Hockey*, Ontario Ministry of Culture and Recreation and Ontario Hockey Council, 1975, pp. 27-28.

Dear Mom and Dad:

I hope that you won't get mad at me for writing this letter, but you always told me never to keep anything back that ought to be brought out into the open. So here goes.

Remember the other morning when my team was playing and both of you were sitting and watching. Well, I hope that you won't get mad at me, but you kind of embarrassed me. Remember when I went after the ball in front of the net trying to score and tripped and fell? I could hear you yelling at me for being so stupid. I was sure embarrassed—a little because I tripped, but a lot because you were yelling.

Then do you remember yelling at me to get back into position? The coach told me to cover the other forward and I couldn't if I listened to you, and while I tried to decide they scored against us. Then you yelled at me for being in the wrong place.

You shouldn't have jumped all over the coach for pulling me off the field. She is a pretty good coach, and a good person, and she knows what she is doing. Besides she is just a volunteer coming down at all hours of the day helping us kids, just because she loves sports.

And then neither of you spoke to me the whole way home. I guess you were pretty sore at me for not getting a goal. I tried awfully hard, but I guess I am a crummy field hockey player. But, I love the game, it is lots of fun being with the other kids and learning to compete. It is a good sport, but how can I learn if you don't show me a good example. And anyhow I thought I was playing field hockey for fun, to have a good time, and to learn good sportsmanship. I didn't know that you were going to get so upset because I couldn't become a star.

Love,

Chris

4
Understanding
Your
Child

Most parents have questions about their child's participation in field hockey. We've taken those questions parents most often ask or should ask and obtained answers from sport physiologists, psychologists, physicians, experienced coaches and parents, and even some young players. The answers attempt to assist you in meeting your responsibilities as parents of a young field hockey player.

PHYSICAL CONCERNS

When is my child ready to play field hockey?

Because children differ so much in their physical and psychological maturity, no one age is best for beginning to play. Parents and coaches, therefore, must rely on their common sense to judge whether or not a particular youngster is ready to participate in a structured field hockey program. One essential element for judging your child's readiness is the interest he or she expresses in participating—this interest must not be the result of adult coercion, however. Typically boys and girls do not find a structured field hockey program to be interesting until they are about 8 years old.

When should youngsters begin competing?

In the hopes of creating superathletes, some parents push their children to practice 2 to 4 hours every day from the time they are 5 to 6 years old. Few children have the natural desire to pursue anything—sports or other activities—with that degree of dedication. When children have their whole life built around a sport, they miss out on other important aspects of growing up. Consequently, they all too often "burn out" or develop resentment for the sport and those adults who pressured them to play.

Field hockey should not demand all of your child's leisure time. Your child should have the opportunity to learn other sports and recreational skills as well as attend to schoolwork and the natural pursuits of youth. Once again, let your child

"This diaper league does create unexpected time outs!"

determine the degree of his or her commitment to USA Junior Field Hockey without pressure from you or the coach.

For most 8-year olds, two or three 1-hour practices per week and one or two games is about right, and 10 or 15 minutes of ball-handling skills practiced at home is recommended per day. The season should not be too long either—6 to 8 weeks is enough. As a child's age, skill, fitness, and interest increase, so too can the length and frequency of practices and matches, as well as the duration of the season, increase.

Should boys and girls be allowed to play hockey on the same and/or opposing teams?

Before puberty there is no reason why girls and boys cannot compete together fairly, but after puberty the story may be different. As boys mature, they become stronger and have a greater ability to run at high speeds, therefore potentially dominating the field hockey game. After puberty, it is recommended that boys and girls play on different teams, unless special rules ensure the equality of play. In the US and other countries, "mixed hockey" is extremely popular.

Does my child need a medical examination prior to the field hockey season?

All children should have a medical examination at least once a year. If your child has not had one this year, just before the season begins is good time to get one. Also, if your child has had a serious injury or illness, a physician should be consulted 'before he or she is permitted to re-enter the field hockey program.

What is the risk of injury to my child?

We know that injuries constitute one of parents' foremost concerns, and rightfully so. Injuries seem to be an inevitable aspect of any rigorous activity, especially one involving as much movement as field hockey does. But because players are relatively closely matched in body size, and high-speed collisions or injuries resulting from being hit with a stick or ball rarely occur, severe injuries such as bone fractures are in-

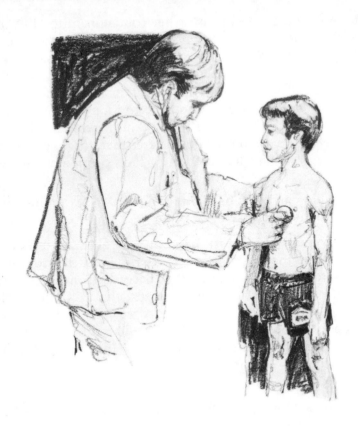

"All children should have a physical examination at least once a year."

frequent. Instead, the majority of injuries in field hockey are the same as would be found in runners—sprains and strains, abrasions, and the occasional bruise. We try to reduce the likelihood and severity of even these relatively minor injuries by exercising basic precautions, such as well-organized practice conditions, adequate facilities, sufficient warm-ups, and proper conditioning.

What happens if my child is injured while playing hockey?

First, we try to make sure all coaches know first-aid procedures for injuries common to field hockey. If a serious injury occurs, the coach will immediately seek medical assistance and then contact you properly.

How can I determine when an injury or illness is sufficiently severe to remove my child from participation?

It comes down to common sense on your part—and a consultation with your physician if you are in doubt. The decision to withhold your child from a practice or match is made more easily when your child's well-being is given precedence over winning.

What should I know about treating sprains and strains?

Sprains and strains are similar types of injuries, because both involve over-stretching or tearing of tissue and internal bleeding. A sprain occurs when the joint is forced beyond its normal range of motion, injuring the soft tissue around it. In contrast, a strain is an injury to the muscle itself and does not involve a bone or joint. With a strain, the pain will be located in the muscle rather than a joint, and swelling is not likely to be as noticeable. In both strains and sprains, the severity of the injury depends on whether the ligaments or muscle tissues are merely overstretched or actually torn. For either injury, the immediate first-aid can be summarized by the word ICE:

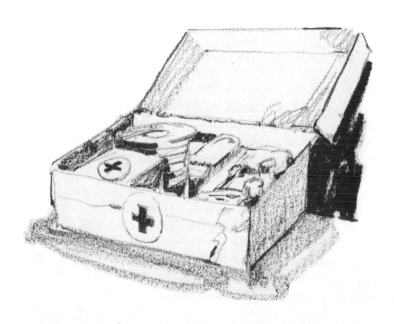

For sprains and strains, the immediate first-aid can be summarized by the word "ICE."

   I Apply Ice or cold to control internal bleeding;
   C Compress with an elastic bandage to help control swelling;
   E Elevate the part to prevent pooling of blood

These immediate steps—the first especially—are generally well known. The confusion arises later regarding the follow-up treatment during the often long, slow recovery. Once the initial bleeding and swelling has stopped, the objective is to stimulate circulation to the injured part to carry away the waste products and aid recovery. This can be achieved by hot, wet applications, but it will also result from the continued application of cold! In fact, the ice method is now thought to be superior because the resulting increase in circulation will last several hours *after* the ice has been removed. The use of ice has the added advantage of helping to reduce pain, enabling the person to move the joint with less discomfort, and thus preventing it from becoming stiff with disuse.

For example, if your youngster sprains a wrist, there may be a noticeable swelling and soreness. As soon as possible, ice should be applied to the injured wrist. One of the best methods is immersing the wrist in ice water. This should be continued for no more than 20 minutes. During the next few days, the wrist should be soaked in ice water three to four times a day for periods of about 15 minutes. After the ice-water treatment, it is very important to exercise the wrist, moving and stretching it through its full range of motion.

Can I help my child's performance through his or her diet?

You sure can. Living as we do in the age of "junk foods" it is all the more important to be informed about our eating patterns. Your child's involvement in USA Junior Field Hockey can provide a useful means of teaching and emphasizing the value of sound nutritional practices, and you can help to establish good lifetime eating habits. You might explain to your youngster that an athlete is in the business of optimizing his or her performance potential. Therefore, calories cannot be wasted on foods of low nutritional value. If your child understands this, he or she will be more likely to make the most of what is eaten, for example, choosing vitamin-packed apples and oranges over sugar-loaded candy or high-calorie, salt-laden potato chips.

How do I know what my child's weight should be?

Some children can obviously afford to lose some fat—and it is good if field hockey is their incentive to do so. When losing excess weight, youngsters should follow a sensible diet which allows them to lose the fat weight gradually—at a rate of no more than 2 pounds per week.

The most effective body weight for athletic competition allows for adequate water and no excessive body fat. We usually make a reasonably accurate visual assessment of a child's need to gain or lose weight. If you remain uncertain about your child's appropriate weight, consult your physician. The physician will measure your child's body fat percentage to determine his or her appropriate body weight for playing hockey or participating in any sport.

Are any special diets or food supplements helpful to young athletes?

There are no miracle foods or wonder supplements—no single food or food group offers an advantage to field hockey players. Because the body's requirements for vitamins, minerals, and calories are provided by a vast array of foods, nutritional needs are best met by a varied, well-balanced diet. Contrary to common belief, athletes do not need exceptional amounts of vitamins, minerals, or proteins. Depending on the type of nutrient, excess quantities are either excreted in the urine or stored in the body at potentially toxic levels. In short, the best diet is a well-balanced diet.

What about the pregame meal?

The most important thing is to ensure that your youngster has eaten long enough before the competition so that the stomach will be empty. There-fore, the final pregame meal should occur no less than 3 hours before the competition. It should consist primarily of carbohydrates, which are most easily digested and converted into energy. By this we don't mean sugary drinks and can-dy! Carbohydrates are found in cereals, breads, grains, fruits, and vegetables. The meals should be low in protein and fat, both of which are slowly digested. Perhaps the most important criterion is that the meal should not devi-ate substantially from the child's usual diet. On the day of the game, the child—complete with nervous stomach—should be allowed to eat familiar foods. Match day is no time for ex-perimentation.

How should my child eat during a tournament?

A day-long tournament presents special problems for meeting nutritional needs. The problem becomes one of maintaining energy levels throughout the day, without having to compete on a full stomach. A promising solution may be to provide cans of liquid meals (such as Nutrament or Sustagen), which the athlete can sip through the day. These products are largely comprised of carbohydrates and are readily digested.

What should players drink during competition?

The other important aspect of nutrition is adequate hydration. It is vital to ensure that fluid loss is replaced throughout the day of competition or practice by *scheduling* frequent drinks of water. The body's thirst mechanism is a delayed response and cannot be depended on to cue the need to drink. And remember, youngsters are likely to forget to drink throughout the day unless they are reminded.

How much rest is enough?

Adults who train daily usually find that they require at least 8 hours of sleep in order to function at their best. A growing child engaged in strenuous athletic training will certainly require 8 to 10 hours of sleep.

PSYCHOLOGICAL CONCERNS

Without a doubt some of the most difficult and challenging problems confronting both the young athlete and parents concern learning how to deal with the intangible psychological factors. Controlling emotions, handling stress, relating to coaches, dealing with winning and losing—even knowing how to behave at matches—all are problems affecting both you and your child. In this section, we attempt to answer some of the common questions about these psychological aspects of your child's participation in USA Junior Field Hockey.

Can field hockey be too stressful for my child?

It may be if your child is made to feel that his or her self-worth depends on field hockey performance. When those things most important to your child—such as love and approval—are contingent on hockey performance, your child is likely to experience high levels of stress. Nevertheless, recent research has shown that for a great majority of children, field hockey is not any more stressful than many other activities in which they participate. When coaches and parents keep winning in proper perspective, field hockey is rarely too stressful.

Isn't it good for children to learn to cope with stress?

Yes, competitive stress can be beneficial as long as it is not overwhelming (resulting in what psychologists call "distress"). Moderate levels of competitive stress can help teach your child how to cope with pressure, to have commitment to purpose, and to value achievement.

But what if my child appears to be distressed or overly stressed?

Begin by talking to your youngster, and perhaps to the coach, to uncover the cause of anxiety. Almost always the anxiety is caused by doubts about how other people will feel about the child if he or she performs poorly, especially those people who mean a great deal to the child—coach, teammates, friends, or parents. If you can help your child to understand that striving to win is important but that his or her worthiness as a person is not determined by a win-loss record, then your child will not find field hockey overly stressful.

How can I help my child to develop the proper attitude toward winning?

Help your youngster to develop realistic expectancies of his or her capabilities in field hockey. This requires, of course, that *you* have realistic expectancies of your child, something parents do not always have. When parents hold excessively high expectancies for their child, they may lead the child into believing him or herself capable of doing more than is actually possible. Children with unrealistically high expectancies are often frustrated in field hockey, for even when they play near their capacity, their aspirations remain unfulfilled. You must help your child to formulate sensible goals so they can derive full enjoyment from field hockey.

What do I say about the ways my child plays hockey?

Sometimes it may seem like everything you say comes out the wrong way. When children know they did not play well, they do not want to be told, "You did just fine." And youngsters who have just lost a game do not want to hear, "It really isn't important." At the moment, it is important to the youngsters and they expect to be permitted the dignity of their unhappiness.

Although parents mean well, these comments seem to be superficial and to reflect a lack of sincerity. Youngsters seem to have a built-in apparatus for detection of "phony" attitudes, and they resent them deeply. When parents are insincere, the child reduces the value of their words and later may be unable to get full satisfaction from deserved praise. In short, be generous with praise and sparing with criticism, but don't be a phony.

"Lost again, eh Son?"

"Yeah, must be hereditary, eh Dad!"

Is there anything else?

Some parents are quick to blame their child for not trying hard enough when he or she fails. It can seem that a failure or loss makes the parents a failure. Embarrassed by a missed opportunity or lost ball, parents will sometimes demean their child publicly, as if to say to observers, "You see, I taught the kid better, but the dummy just won't do as I say." This is a tragic mistake. The parent loses the respect of the coach, other parents, and most importantly, of his or her own child.

People often say that sports are a good way to teach children useful lessons about how to win and lose in life. How can I help my child in this regard?

Psychologists have learned that the causes you and your child assign to the experiences he or she has are important in shaping the child's personality and future behaviors. These causes are called attributions. When children lose, some parents are reluctant to blame their child and quick to blame others—the coach, the referee, other team members, or even luck or fate. Never is the child faulted for failing to succeed: It is always due to someone or something else. Parents who express such attributions often unwittingly foster the attitude in their children that they are never responsible for their own behavior. Children begin to view the world as if what happens to them is the result of forces beyond their control. Such a view is unhealthy.

On the other hand, when parents help their children to accurately interpret the causes of winning and losing—to distinguish between external causes and their own ability or effort—children develop an attitude that they are both responsible for their actions and in control over much of their environment. This is a healthy attitude.

Can my child care too much about field hockey?

It is always good for children to be committed to such activities as hockey, to care about how they perform, and to push themselves to achieve excellence. Developing commitment is a useful lesson in later life, too. Let your child care and then care with your child. But sometimes children care too much: They equate their self-worth with winning and losing, they mope around the house for a week after the loss, and they ignore their other responsibilities. When this occurs, it is your responsibility to help your child put things into perspective.

Should parents attend practices and games?

Attending a few practices during the season so you can see what your child is learning is a good idea. We don't think that always attending them is good, however. We encourage you to attend all your youngster's matches, but if your presence appears to make your child nervous, it may be a good idea not to go to the games until the child gains more confidence in his or her playing abilities. Ask your child if he or she would like you to come!

What if my child misbehaves?

Throughout this booklet we have placed most of the burden for a successful sports program on the adults—you, the parent, and we, the coaches. But sometimes children misbehave—they break the rules, are uncooperative, uncontrollable, and irresponsible. Children do have obligations to their parents and to the coach when they become part of a USA Junior Field Hockey team. They are responsible for cooperating with coaches and teammates, for being prompt to practice and games, and for their own conduct. When children misbehave, the coach has some right and responsibility to discipline them. Ultimately, however, the responsibility for disciplining belongs to you, and you must use it wisely.

What if my child wants to quit playing field hockey?

Listen to your child and try to find out why. Although there is little value in forcing your youngster to continue, for the child's sake, encourage him or her to finish out the season as part of a commitment to something started. If the child doesn't want to, recognize the fact that he or she may not share the other youngsters' interest in the game.

What do I do if my child is unhappy with the coach?

If it seems to be a serious problem, try to understand your child's position. But before you side with your child, discuss the problem with the coach to see it from the coach's point of view. Then attempt to help your child work out a solution with the coach.

Many field hockey programs recognize players through such means as selecting outstanding players, having recognition dinners, and giving trophies and other tangible awards. Are these practices desirable?

Giving children recognition for their achievements is fine as long as the rewards are not extravagant and are awarded fairly. Children wish to be recognized for their accomplishments just as adults do. The danger in these practices occurs when children lose perspective about the significance of such recognition. Some youngsters assume a false sense of importance from such recognition, behaving like prima donnas. Others lose interest in striving to achieve unless significant, tangible rewards are at stake. You need to help your child to see these rewards merely as recognition for past accomplishments, not future successes. Your child needs to realize that these extrinsic rewards are only one benefit of sport participation and that the more important outcomes are the intrinsic rewards of fun and satisfaction.

905185